D0920146

THE PORCELAIN APES
OF MOSES MENDELSSOHN

Jean Nordhaus

MILKWEED EDITIONS

© 2002, Text by Jean Nordhaus
All rights reserved. Except for brief quotations in critical articles or reviews, no part of this book may be reproduced in any manner without prior written permission from the publisher: Milkweed Editions, 1011 Washington Avenue South, Suite 300, Minneapolis, Minnesota 55415.
(800) 520-6455
www.milkweed.org / www.worldashome.org

Published 2002 by Milkweed Editions
Printed in the United States of America
Cover and interior design by Dale Cooney
Interior art courtesy of the Jewish National and University Library, Jerusalem
The text of this book is set in Centaur
02 03 04 05 06   5 4 3 2 1
First Edition

Special underwriting for this book was generously provided by
Brenda Wehle and John Carroll Lynch.

Milkweed Editions, a nonprofit publisher, gratefully acknowledges support from the Bush Foundation; General Mills Foundation; Marshall Field's Project Imagine with support from the Target Foundation; McKnight Foundation; Minnesota State Arts Board through an appropriation by the Minnesota State Legislature and a grant from the National Endowment for the Arts, and a grant from the Wells Fargo Foundation Minnesota; A Resource for Change technology grant from the National Endowment for the Arts; St. Paul Companies, Inc.; Target Stores; and generous individuals.

Library of Congress Cataloging-in-Publication Data

Nordhaus, Jean, 1939–
    The porcelain apes of Moses Mendelssohn / Jean Nordhaus.— 1st ed.
      p. cm.
    ISBN 1-57131-414-8 (pbk. : alk. paper)
      1. Mendelssohn, Moses, 1729–1786—Poetry. 2. Jewish philosophers—Poetry. 3. Jews—Germany—Poetry. 4. Jewish authors—Poetry. 5. Philosophers—Poetry. 6. Authors—Poetry.
    I. Title.

PS3564.O558 P67 2002
811'.54—dc21   2001044365

This book is printed on acid-free paper.

For Ted and Hannah

THE PORCELAIN APES
OF MOSES MENDELSSOHN

. . . under Frederic the Great every Jew had to purchase, on the occasion of his marriage, a certain amount of china from the newly established royal china factory in Berlin, and that not according to his own choice, but that of the manager of the factory, who made use of the opportunity to get rid of things otherwise unsalable. Thus Moses Mendelssohn, a man even then generally known and honoured, became possessed of twenty life-sized china apes, some of which are still preserved in the family.

—Sebastian Hensel, THE MENDELSSOHN FAMILY

THE PORCELAIN APES
OF MOSES MENDELSSOHN

HE ENTERS BERLIN THROUGH
THE ROSENTHAL GATE

Far easier for a rich man
to enter heaven. Say

you've been walking for days,
fourteen years old, a brimming cup—

away from Dessau and the ghetto,
everything you know. You follow

your teacher, a hunger, a love.
With your bad shoes, a stammer,

a slight hump, will you be the camel
that squeezes through? Suppose you've been

walking all night and you come to that gate.
(All the rest are closed for you.)

New sun striking ancient stone, so bright
it blinds. Now set a sentry

in your path, a sphinx
who questions you. Parable

insists on this, though what she asks—
what you reply—will not survive.

And what to set above that portal
on the doorpost of your story? How shall I enter,

a Jew?—Through words, the smallest
opening. *May they be*

acceptable. In the sentry
book of 1743 is written:

Today there passed through the Rosenthal Gate
six oxen, seven swine, and one Jew.

[handwritten annotations: impossible; Many Jews entered society through education; Liturgy in Christianity AND Judaism; watched exclusion → dehumanizing]

A BOWL ON MY BACK

I was born with a frame
so twisted even goblins
would have cast me out.

But my own mother kept me
and sang me songs. My father
carried me on his strong shoulders

to the rabbis, and a good woman
loved me—my Fromet—so frightened
when I first came to call, but she swayed

to my side when I told my fable
of the man who took the hump (which God
had prepared) on himself so his wife

could be beautiful. Ugliness
is the stepchild of evil, a mal-
proportion of parts.

But the life of the mind
is seamless, rare, brighter

than silver, culmination

of the body's longing.
Man is an instrument
of string and bone.

Yet from my name the wind
made music—Men-
delssohn. The notes remain.

Coda

The hump, too, prospered. → prejudice
It burrowed and fed   continues
in forgotten hollows, gorged
on scraps of garbled prophesy.
Buried, it died and rose again
to bloom in twisted letters
from the chimneys, alephs and gimels,
angels of smoke, the small voices
calling for mercy where there was none.

HE LEARNS GERMAN

[handwritten annotation: Jews most easily assimilated into German culture, ironically]

It mocks you, baring its teeth
in an ape grin. Behind
this fence of syllables
you are locked in, locked out;
for the book of its rules
is sealed with a padlock.
Who steals this grammar
will be damned himself.

Covert under blankets
at night with small strokes
you unriddle the combinations.
You work your way through a syntax
of hammers and traps, trip
the pins and latches and escape—

Will you open this door, Jew?
Will you enter the house
as a burglar and make it your home?

[handwritten annotation: learning a language takes away a part of your original identity]

Go in. It is too late now
to turn back. Step into the castle

and take up its cause as your own.

You will need these runes
to build a thesis, mend a quarrel, } *objectives*
raise a treatise, and chastise a king.

— learns German
↳ for unity; communication
— thru language, he can
connect to a larger culture

THE WEEKLY LOAF

Every week I buy a fresh loaf of bread
and score it with lines
marking the seven days
so as not to feast now   *self-restraint*
and go hungry by Sabbath.
Then I go about my work
with an eager mind. I brush

my black pen through the words   *writing a*
of others, I teach myself   *way out*
patience. I push   *of isolation*
through the pages at night,
hunting glimmers
and clues. If the mind
can nourish itself,

the strength of the body
will follow. This I believe—
as an answer must flow
from the shape of a question,
as the syllogism of the tree
assumes the sun. Each man's life

is a loaf he is given

to hoard or spend
as he will. But the mind
is a chasm, an empty
vessel, a rift in the earth
a wind blows through. To feed
this glutton, I am frugal,
I busy myself with the law. I stint

to make a generosity
of what I am, a fullness
out of want. The good Lord
made the earth in seven days.
I carve these lines in the crust
like commandments and follow them well,
so as not to exceed each day's measure.

ISOLATION

SILK => tediousness
⌐ mechanical, as well

The vote of the Has it
writer => been
perverted.

Tone of this
poem much more
pessimistic than
Whitman's "Noiseless
Spider"

hump

Whitman

like baptism

internal to
eternal
⌐ just like
the
spider

because
the state

downfall

Mendelssohn
dehumanized
for a material
profit

more
guilt

alienation
or
atonement

silk like
writing

more
guilt

Silkworms
boiled alive to
get I continuous
strand, b/c the moth eats a hole
in cocoon

I keep the books in a silk factory
for my employer, Herr Bernhard. The work
is not hard, but I suffer, feeling I was made
for finer things. All day
I hunch like a spider over my ledger.
I dip my pen into the well—
this pen that could be used to spar or sing—
drawing out of the black pool a line, thin
as a thread, fine as a baby's hair.
This columned page for warp
and woof, it is my own death
I weave here, winding myself
in a shroud of silk. Soon I shall sleep
the sleep of the worm, without thought
or dream. Sometimes I wonder
that so many tiny deaths
are daily woven into cloth so thin,
so light, it seems almost a substance
of the spirit. Then I dip my pen
for penance in the well and plod again
across the rows of numbers
until every shred and pennyworth
is accounted for.

I DREAMT OF A CHILD

I never knew I'd had,
for he had lost his tribe
and wandered in the wilderness
alone. His salty tears
collected in a pool so deep,
I dropped a pebble in
but could not hear it speak.
I sent my lone voice
after him. An echoing
chorus answered me.

[handwritten annotation: subconcious? telling → most italics used for thought process]

THE STAMMER

We are two-minded, my tongue and I.
It is always like this: I mean
to say *That house is tall.*
or *God is one.* But the tongue   involuntary
has another opinion. It wants

to be heard. We are like Mishnah,
two sparrows disputing
a morsel of law. I grapple
with my tongue as Jacob
wrestled with the angel

for a word. From this clash
of intentions I've learned
to hold back, to listen:
the voice at my shoulder when I
try to speak, saying

Wait. The tongue
is a caged beast, an animal
wild to escape. Compel it,
and it will elude you. Released,

it will yield to your lightest

desire. Soft, and the sounds that need
to speak themselves will flow.
Be gentle, and the words
will come like deer
to water or a woman to love.

THERE IS NO REASON IN IT

"mandatory"
love poem

No reason at all. This morning
I walked out in early fog, and as the sun
burned through, an owl flew by,
feathering home from a night
of hunting, low along the breast of land.
No theorem, no system of thought
can explain how I long to be near her,
how my blood leaps like a fish
at the sound of her name.

MY FATHER'S BLESSING

When I set out from Dessau
with my father's blessing
and my mother's golden coin,
I knew the coin would buy me food,
a bed, a brazier's glow, but I
could not assess the good
my father's gift would buy.
Berlin in winter quakes with cold,
turns breath to gauze. Some days
my fingers would not hold a pen.
I had only his words and the fire
in my brain, fed by the turning
of pages. Faith is a cauldron
that consumes its children;
love, the tile stove giving
steady heat. He lifted his arms
as if he were the voyager,
warming his hands at a grate,
unfurled the blessing like a shawl,
and covered me. Today I bend
my knees and take it on.

A PURCHASE OF PORCELAIN

Because the king
decrees that every Jew
must buy his wedding-right
in unsold porcelain
from the royal china works,

he stands, an amorous Jew,
gazing at luminous
suns and moons arrayed
on cloths of velvet blue,
earth that has married fire twice,

that has been shaped and named
for what it comprehends: *sherbets, salads,*
gravies, desserts. He lifts a platter fine
as alabaster in cathedral windows:
salvation, the passage of light

through bone. *Ah, but*
not for you, the store-man says.
Closeted, in shipping crates
are pieces no one else will buy:

baboon fops in feathered caps,

chimpanzees in petticoats.
Visitors will later testify,
his home was comfortable,
despite the china apes
peering from every corner.

FROMET

Like stars revolving in their circles,
I move through the round of my duties
keeping track of what we have: linens
and candles, children and spoons.
Pennies, anniversaries. My husband teases
that I even count the raisins
and almonds I set on my table.
But who will count them otherwise?
Doesn't God number the stars
he sets out in the bowl at night
and puts away each morning
so that none may be snuffed out beyond
his ken? The good housekeeper knows
if we are careful in the smallest things,
the large will suffice. That's why we tally
the names of the dead and why we
give thanks daily for the living, the little
we own, even for the emptiness
that fills our lungs.

HE PETITIONS FOR THE RIGHT
TO RESIDE IN BERLIN

Maimonides, beloved teacher,
make me understand. Am I
to seek permission from
the king, a man like me
who sweats and prays,
whose words come steeped
in the smell of his lunch,
to set my Jewish rump
upon his public benches? *When the gates*
are opened and men enter, you have said,
their souls will enjoy repose, their eyes
be gratified, and even their bodies,
after all toil and strain, will be refreshed.
Teach me, honored friend, the antonyms
for *pride,* the homonyms for *shame*
and *sham,* and how the question
modifies the questioner. Truly,
I am perplexed.

HOW HE WROTE HIS *PHAEDON, OR THE IMMORTALITY OF THE SOUL*

It was simple. I was sitting
in the courtyard of Herr Grab's house
waiting to deliver a bolt of silk
when it came to me, complete—
like a suit of clothing to the mind
of a tailor before he cuts the cloth:

Socrates, I thought, had not gone
far enough. So I picked up
the thread where he dropped it
and followed it down,
through winding hallways
to the underworld. There

I found that ancient gadfly,
homely and voluble as a crow,
that son of a midwife,
still bristling with questions.
How could he begrudge the world
a bit more talk, he who had died

from the feet up? And so we nudged
the thread along to weave
a premise for the soul: no matter
could be simpler. Before he swallowed
his brimming cup of hemlock
and was swallowed up again himself

in folds of thought so dense
I could not follow, he dropped
a black feather, this quill
I used to trace our conversation.
Three days of frenzy
and the book was done.

I had only to receive his words
and write them down.
It's harder—believe me—
to love your neighbor
or remember on your deathbed
to repay a debt.

THE TOLL FOR A JEW

I traveled many days
but at the gates of Dresden
I could go no farther without paying.

The tolls for a Jew and a pig
are the same; a Jew
who styles himself

a German philosopher
is charged no more
than a Polish cow,

and must I pay
my weight in shame
to shuffle a bag of meat

and fur from one patch of soil
to another? There as here,
the dirt is bare, stamped

with tracks of men
and livestock, clean and

unclean, cloven and whole.

Yet when I step across
the bar, adding my print
to the rough design, they tax

this nimble pod (contrived
for travel as the hand for
touch, the tongue for speech)

as if my human feet were hooves
and I, who would live
without harm, the walking devil.

AN ISRAELITE IN WHOM THERE IS NO GUILE

Johann Kaspar Lavater, phrenologist,
Swiss deacon, former friend and guest
to Mendelssohn, translates a Christian tract
that "proves"—through miracles—his faith correct
and dedicates it to his Jewish friend,
"an Israelite in whom there is no guile,"
whose cranial bumps and dents reveal, he claims,
a noble soul—

> *I've probed the hills and valleys*
> *of your skull, traced with thumb*
> *and calipers the shelves of bone*
> *around your eyes, deep wells*
> *hiding flashes of a great fish*
> *circling in that basin.*
>
> *(If I could catch*
> *and land this specimen: Oh, hungry,*
> *hungry for a prize. I'd*
> *bring him to the table*
> *of the church. My trophy.) Listen,*

friend, I bring you
proof: fishes and loaves, flesh
and wine. Heralds, footprints
on water. Stars
and resurrections.

          Come.

—————

The Jew explores his noble bumps and dents,
his pools of wisdom and diplomacy,
for how can he reply without offense
to those with whom he dwells in tremulous
peace? He hesitates, then lifts his pen:

    Spare me, friend, such missionary
    love. It hides a hook.
    ~~Can I defend my father's~~ faith
    without blaspheming
    yours? It's hard enough
    to slip my skin

    through nature's nets
    and traps. Miracles abound
    in every faith. But what

is more miraculous than this:
that one might taste another
in his otherness and let him be?

THE BREAK

Sometimes he sits so still in his chair, it's like a ghost in the room. *Moses, I say. Moyshe—Where are you? Where have you gone?*—'Daheim,' he says, *I'm hunting mushrooms in the woods near Dessau,* or *I'm standing in the rain outside my cousin Itka's house.*

He never used to talk about the ghetto. He'd put it behind him. But what's behind will walk ahead of you all your life, my mother used to say. No one invents himself from the shoes up. No one breathes into his own dust. Some days he shuffles from room to room in his dressing gown, fiddles with his models or the chimney flue—a man who used every second. He counts the roof tiles on the house across the street. But one thing he doesn't do. He doesn't sit at his desk anymore, writing books. The doctor has forbidden that.

So, my good husband has time on his hands—and he's thinking, but not the kind of thoughts he used to have, the kind you can write down. It was his free-minded friends who started him off, helping him publish his papers, filling him up with talk of a new age.

The doctor thinks Moses ~~is angry,~~ that straining to
be larger than his enemies has drained his nerve. But I
think he is disappointed with the world, grieving for his
own ambition, all that studying, the bridge he hoped to
build with his own being. I could have told him. Moses,
I could have said. . . . But who would listen?

YIDDISH

Sometimes when my mother
opened her mouth to speak, a shoe
tumbled out or a featherless
chicken that settled its head
on my pillow, claw-feet
clenched in prayer.

That's when I learned to fear sleep
and to watch the tongue for danger,
to throw scraps of paper
over the rail and watch
them fall, each fluttering
word a white dove.

Now I pluck them back
and bury them until
they bloom again on the tip
of my tongue and rhyme:
    The kiss and the pillow.
    The tree and the plum.
    A house built of wood

and others, like stanzas, a village
of stanzas. A school. A bridge.
The song running under it. Quick
as a scale. The *sofer*'s long
black coat turned inside out,
patched with diminutives,

basted with stitching
of every color. I try it on.
It fits me perfectly.
The syllables fit in my mouth
    like smoke in the chimney,
    like milk in a thimble,
    the child in its grave.

DEATH HAS KNOCKED AT MY DOOR

Dear Thomas,

faith never rested

and robbed me of a child, which has lived but eleven innocent months; but God be praised, her short life was happy and full of bright promise. My friend, the dear child did not live these eleven months in vain. Her mind had even in that short time made quite an astonishing progress; from a little animal that wept and slept, she grew into the bud of a reasoning creature. . . . She showed pity, hatred, love, and admiration, she understood the language of those who spoke, and endeavored to make known her thoughts to them. . . . I cannot believe that God has set us on His earth like foam on the wave. . . .

Moses Mendelssohn

From Mendelssohn's letter of May 1, 1764, to his friend Thomas Abbt.

THE GHETTO RAISED ME

All the clocks of Europe pause
and turn back at that gate.
Centuries wait in the doorways
in caracul hats. They'll sell you
a bridle, a candle, a coat.
No mingled thread. No green
escape. When I was a boy,
I walked those tangled lanes
and every house and corner
called my name. Yet in my heart
I hid a secret home, a place
where I was bound, where I
belonged. The ghetto raised me,
rocked me in old mysteries,
honed my mind with riddles,
bid me: *Stay!* Does the yolk
tell the egg it is happy
in its jacket—safe, con-
tained? Skin is the only coat
a man cannot remove.

integrity?

HEBREW

By the light of this alphabet
I learned to read: earth and
water, morning and night
slipped through the prism
of meaning, chiseled a path
into stone. On the scroll
of creation, a nation of shepherds
set out—dark staves wandering
across the sand; above and below
in flocks, the drifting vowels.

I became translator, shuttling
between two worlds, carrying
down from the mountain, up
from the well, a text running backward
through rain to the waters' beginning: Pentateuch:
teuch meaning vessel or tool; and *five:*
the fingers of my human hand,
so like the ape's but bending
what it touches to its use, blade
and feather, pen of polished bone.

Mendelssohn translated Hebrew bible into German} persecuted by Rabbis for this

THE RABBI OF FIRTH DECREES THE EXCOMMUNICATION OF ANYONE READING THE GERMAN PENTATEUCH OF MOSES MENDELSSOHN

Bound body and mind to the law,
winding the leather straps, I wear
my clothing black, my hair unshorn. *mourning, dark*
When I give myself to God
I hold nothing back. The Holy Word
conceived in flame, recorded
on the hide of animals, must
not walk naked on this earth.
Lovely as a bride, it must be clothed
in satin, crowned with silver, marched
with ceremony through the aisles. For man
is a field of departures, flinging himself
away; God, the enclosure where nothing
is lost; we, the keepers of His cups
and scrolls, His words and sacred silences.
If many paths may lead to God,
then truth's a dry bone any dog *for anyone*
can chew. Pure reason is a wilderness *& everyone*

unbound. For when we gaze into the mirror
of the past, we see our faces
clearly, but the future is an open
door and gives back no reflection.

HE RENTS A GARDEN

I've leased a garden plot
on Spandau Street,
shelter for my children
from the street boys' gibes and taunts.
Here I sat one afternoon
and watched an insect
tiny as a grain of sand
traverse a continent
no wider than my hand,
waving delicate feelers,
steering by touch. Today my daughter
Brendel split a silver pod
and fastened that enormous wing
upon her nose. When a thought
is launched, who knows
where it may land?

} needs
   protection

A GAME OF CHESS: TWO VIEWS

after the lithograph by S. Meier

At first glance, Lavater and Mendelssohn
confer above the board like warring fates,
be-yarmulked Jew and long-boned clergyman
subsumed in shadows. Each man contemplates
the field of light and dark squares, while a third,
the playwright Lessing, coiffed like an English judge,
presides with the disinterest of a god
who hangs above the battlefield to watch.
A woman with a tray steps through the doorway
from the room beyond, her eyes cast down—
not to spill a drop of tea or shake
the cups. She must not interrupt and they
do not look up, because the Hebrew queen
has seized Christ's knight and placed the king in check.

———————

Look closer now. They've pushed the board aside,
an open book between them. Lavater
leans forward, one hand on the page, the other
on M's sleeve, as if he would persuade
the Jew. Lessing, scowling, looks askance

at Lavater. Only the woman remains
as she was, with covered head and downcast glance,
her figure graceful as an ampersand's
against the kitchen's light. In time her firebrand
daughter will ignite a conflagration
with her passionate heart and rough contempt
for custom. But tonight the woman is intent
on keeping balance, and her concentration
never wavers from the task at hand.

UPON HEARING FANNY MENDELSSOHN'S MUSIC PERFORMED AT MOUNT VERNON COLLEGE IN WASHINGTON, D.C.

Counting cups and spoons,
correcting a child, stitching
at cantatas in the intervals
between birth pangs and samovars,
could she have imagined us, expectant
on gray folding chairs beneath the benefactors'
portraits—other women's ancestors? And knowing this,

would she have penned one measure more
or served her household gods
with less perfection?
She died at the keyboard—at home—
havoc racing down the neurons
like a fugue to overflow in one
dark chord: *Walpurgisnacht,*

her brother's music, scored
for the feast of abandon. Each life
pulses, note by note, as lived, in measures—

neither less, nor more complete
for *Lieder* slipped like beads
along the abacus of days, a word, a breath
expanding in its resonance beyond all reason.

I DREAMT THAT WE WERE IN THE DESERT

and the people cried for water.
I raised my staff—it was my arm
and at the end, a blossom
of my flesh. I broke
the branch and with it
struck the rock
and what came flowing
was not water but a stream
of melody so beautiful
the people wept to hear.
They stretched themselves
along its bank to sleep,
and as they slept
I woke.

Outsider

ABRAHAM AT *MORGENSTUNDEN*

In the stillness before the day begins
the sounds in the house are few.
I hear my mother's voice
downstairs in the kitchen,
the clank of the stove grate
turning the ashes. My father

is strict, but funny.
He never tells us what is true.
He answers a question
with a story and asks what it means,
how you should act, say, if you
find a sack of money on Spandau Street
and don't know whose it is.

His voice is so low, we have to hush
to hear him. When he stammers,
we have to wait. There's a china ape
in the corner with a cape and a sword
and sometimes my father asks *him*.

Yesterday we heard the story of Plato's cave;
today, of father Abraham (that's my name too),
who would have sacrificed the son
he loved out of obedience to God.
But what if God had not changed his mind?
What if the ram had not appeared?

The window is behind me.
I can see our shadows on the wall.
That's how I know the sun is up.
My father's shadow is big as God
and there are the children of Israel—
my sister—there—and Joseph,
and the bronze calf-model on the sill.

Comparing

And there I am. Every time I
wiggle my head, the head on the wall
moves too. That makes me laugh.
I smell Marta's tea cakes in the oven
and I hear my small dog, Pharaoh,
whining at the kitchen door.

THE ROPE WAS INNOCENT

and the ass, the two menservants
below on the plain, the ram,
the wood, the knife,
the fire. The pit, the rack,
the bullwhip—all the instruments

were innocent: iron slept
cold in the ground. But love
was not innocent. It was love
who gave the order and love
who obeyed, who carried and stacked

the wood, offered wrists and
ankles for the binding. Love
prepared the fire and raised
the knife, and it was love
who lowered it. Bless the animals,

who live without mercy: the ape
with her beautiful breasts,
nursing her young, the tethered
ram, and the ass grazing there

in the lowlands—little woolly ass

who cannot pray, who hears only
the braying of wind in the grass
and when death comes with its smell
of lion, answers, *Here am I*,
and falls to its knees without wonder.

certain
innocence

FROM HERE
↳ living in 2 diff worlds &
the contradiction it has

THE BODY TAX

Winter.
The oil in the lamp
burns low. The ghost-flame
gutters that sustained itself
these many years, and I must pause
before the custom house
to pay my toll in pain.
How hard it is to translate
water into steam. To pass
from one state to another is work,
and to die is an arduous birthing.
The mind can move
through space and time
without impediment. The body,
stubborn cow, must pay
to pass, must set its print
upon the earth and be
ploughed under. Fifty-seven
years I've walked this rutted
wagon road—one foot
in the track of reason, one in prayer.
Now I see the vanishing point
where parallels converge.

*classicly Jewish
(Hannukah)*

no more livelheart

❧ 47 ❧

JANUARY 4, 1786

There are many roads to prayer,
but only one gate to the City.
I have passed through.

Knows his own destiny
↳ fulfilled

THE STRANGER FROM DESSAU

*When things perish, they do not pass into nothingness but are
dissolved into their elements.*

They called me Mendel's son
and, yes, I was his son,
but the Hebrew seal
I set below my name read:
Moses, the Stranger

from Dessau. Strange things
happen in this world. Gods
are stolen, babies
suckled into tyrants,
but what could be less

likely than a ghetto boy
with twisted back and
clumsy tongue, to lead
his landsmen from their gabled
bondage? My father

copied out inscriptions
from the Pentateuch.

They stuffed the phrases
into tiny boxes, fastened them
to doorjambs and above

their eyes in prayer.   *play on last*
My name is Moses.   *name*
I was Mendel's son. I walked
from Dessau with its tangled
ghetto into Europe's glimmering

age of light. And I
am buried here among
the shades, a citizen
in one republic
darker than the pages

of a book forever closed.
Dissolved into my elements:
a mound of dust, a spill of bones,
words bound in a narrow box.
And what can be stranger than that?

JERUSALEM

Ladder and well
I know that I will never
reach that land
where word and world
are one, where a man
can lean out
like a ladle over water
and see clear to the bottom.

Stars and grains of sand
were promised, countless
generations. But I tell you
to be chosen is to live forever
in a state of longing.

And if I build the road
cobble by cobble,
I will never arrive. It is here
I must live, among chipped stones
and flints, weapons of need,
the mind's makeshift inventions.

Jewel in the eye,

JERUSALEM

Ruby of

Salem,

*Ladder stretching from
the floor of loneliness,*

Milk of memory
and mercy's tide.

I have set my lookout here
upon the mountain
where I watch a fox-cloud
crossing over, blue

as smoke. With all my gaze
I follow it—

Jerusalem.

THE GRIN

Man has learned it from his
kin: the monkey, chimpanzee,
baboon. In the theater
of the face, a living
rictus is unveiled, scarlet

curtains opening upon a row
of tombstone teeth as if
to show that all I am
and build will come
to jest. Wherever reason

is suspended and the self
switched off—in stool,
in labor, love, inebria,
the grin appears: *Memento
mori* of the animal

I am. In time's museum
or on a palace wall,
Beauty will arrange her face
in a serene half-smile,

closing her famous lips

over black wind. She
seals them as if she
would swallow a word,
but in the end
the grin will out.

Can nolonger contain it

THE PORCELAIN APES
OF MOSES MENDELSSOHN

Of course I was angry at first.
Despite what you think, I am not a rich man—
to have to pay (and dearly, too)
for these grotesques?

The manager thought it a fine joke—
selling apes to the Jew, beasts
to the beast. But I am not ashamed.
The dumb beasts have less vanity
than many a man who vaunts himself
created in God's image. With time, I've grown fond
of my porcelain pets. They ask nothing more
than a corner to stand in. And sometimes at night,
one will gleam out from the shadows,
bow and give me a wink as I pass.
For if you embrace your afflictions
and call them your own, they will become

your blessings. I've even
given them names: This bent one
is My Hump. And that one

with his hands beside his open mouth
I've dubbed The Stammerer.
The one with the dagger
is Lavater. And this one
is known to the family
as Frederick the Great.

I could go on, but you understand . . .

56

Handwritten annotations:

Biography of the apes
4) like Mendelssohn

⟹ made Mendelssohn purchase the apes

showing limits
↳ only God is unlimited

very literal
↳ purely descriptions

the beasts are inside

not just Mendelssohn afflicted, makes it universal.

God curses Mendelsohn
w/ apes, but blesses him @ the same time
w/ the ability to accept them ⟹ shows
the duality of God ⟹ Good + Bad ←

THOU SHALT MAKE NO GRAVEN IMAGE

If man is the likeness of God
and the ape is the likeness of man,
what shall be said of the face and shape
of the creator?

I am a scholar, not a farmer.
I have no cows or pigs. But
like the man in the folktale
whose house was too small,
I brought the beasts inside.

Moses Mendelssohn (left) and Lutheran theologian Johann Caspar Lavater "confer above the board like warring fates." Observing is the writer and dramatist Gotthold Ephraim Lessing, a close friend of Mendelssohn who shared his love of chess. "Look closer now. They've pushed the board aside, / an open book between them. . . ." Lithograph by S. Maier after a painting by Moritz Oppenheim, 1856.

AFTERWORD

I first came across Moses Mendelssohn when I was a graduate student in German literature. He was the prototype for the noble Jew, Nathan the Wise, in Gotthold Ephraim Lessing's play of that name. Lessing knew Mendelssohn through chess and as part of a group of young men promoting the use of German at a time when most educated Germans—including Frederick the Great—thought it more elegant to write in French. As such, Mendelssohn played a small but important role in the German Enlightenment and in the development of German literature. With Lessing's help, Mendelssohn began publishing philosophical essays and articles— among these an unfavorable review of a book of King Frederick's poetry. When attacked, Mendelssohn offered the following defense: "Writing poetry is like bowling, and whoever bowls, be he king or peasant, must have the pinboy tell him his score." Frederick later retaliated by refusing to approve Mendelssohn's nomination to the newly established Royal Academy.

I was to come upon Mendelssohn again many years later while doing research on Felix Mendelssohn's sister Fanny. Mendelssohn family biographies inevitably

before
mechanized
bowling alleys
back men
set the
pins

begin with grandfather Moses, whose life, in these
tellings, has the mythic density of folktale: a poor boy
(born in the ghetto, the gifted son of a humble Torah
scribe) goes off to Berlin to seek his fortune. Although
visited with physical affliction (he is a tiny fellow with
a hump and a stammer so pronounced he must ask
others to read his papers for him), he prevails through
superior wit and virtue—and through his linguistic
gifts—overcoming numerous ordeals to become one of
the most revered intellectuals of his time. The accounts
of these ordeals acquainted me with some of the more
Byzantine facets of eighteenth-century anti-Jewish
regulations, including the incident from which this
collection derives its title.

Most people, if they've heard of Moses Mendelssohn
at all, know him as the grandfather of the composer,
or else as "the Jewish Socrates"—the spiritual grand-
father of the Jewish Enlightenment movement known
as *Haskalah*. In ultrareligious circles he is disparaged
as a secularist whose liberal ideas led Europe's ghetto-
ized Jews toward assimilation on the one hand, and the
disaster of the Holocaust on the other. For better or
worse, he was the first Jew to publish a book in German.

When he arrived in Berlin, the fourteen-year-old

Moses set about providing himself with the secular education forbidden by the rabbis. He taught himself languages (English, French, German, Greek), literature, philosophy, and the sciences, supporting himself, mea- *Independence* gerly at first, as a scribe and tutor, and later (and for the remainder of his life) as bookkeeper and, finally, partner in a silk factory. Although citizenship was not an option for Jews of his era, he was eventually granted "limited protected" status under the Prussian laws regulating Jewish life. This gave him the right to live in Berlin without continual fear of arbitrary expulsion.

Mendelssohn's early writings included a metaphysical paper that won him a prize (over fellow competitor Immanuel Kant) from the Berlin Academy of Science. Fame arrived with the publication in 1767 of his *Phaedon,* a free translation of Plato's *Phaedo,* which Mendelssohn had revised and expanded, in dialogue form, to include the latest philosophical arguments for the immortality of the soul. The book was translated into over thirty languages, and intellectuals throughout Europe made pilgrimage to Berlin to meet its author and gather for *immensly popular* conversation in his home.

Success occasioned Mendelssohn's most difficult public moment. One of his visitors, a Swiss clergyman

and phrenologist named Johann Kaspar Lavater, thought
to enhance his reputation by making a famous convert.
His published challenge placed Mendelssohn (who des-
pite his liberal views remained an observant Jew) in an
extremely delicate position and unleashed a storm of
anti-Semitism that shook his meliorist faith in man and
reason to the point that he ceased writing for seven years.

When he again took up his pen, he turned his
queries inward, toward specifically Jewish themes and
issues—how to reconcile Judaism with the humanistic
ideas of the Enlightenment, how to help his isolated
coreligionists gain access to the surrounding secular
culture. He translated the Pentateuch into German
(using the Hebrew alphabet and borrowing freely from
Martin Luther). He also wrote a treatise entitled
Jerusalem, arguing for the separation of church and state
and presenting Judaism as a religion consonant with
reason, aimed at legislating behavior rather than dic-
tating a specific doctrine. He acted as a generous inter-
mediary and spokesman on behalf of tolerance in gen-
eral and of Jewish civil rights in particular.

Mendelssohn was not a metaphysician or theologian
of the first rank. Whatever his limitations as a thinker,
however, all who came in contact with him recognized

him as a man of luminous humanity and high moral intelligence, who embodied in his person the best of the Enlightenment faith in reason and the dignity of man. He struggled mightily throughout his life to achieve a synthesis between secular and religious values but never fully resolved the ironies of his own situation. Of Mendelssohn's six surviving children, four converted to Christianity.

I confess here to a few liberties. Felix's father Abraham was ten at the time of Moses' death and would not have been present at the daily lessons Moses held for his older children. Then there is the troubling matter of Moses' attitude toward Yiddish. Like so many educated German Jews, he did indeed find Yiddish an embarrassment, although he appears to have used it in his correspondence with his wife. There is no record of his having had a change of heart after his conflict with Lavater. I have had to change it for him.

ACKNOWLEDGMENTS

Earlier versions of many of the poems in this book appeared in *Critical Quarterly, Jewish Women's Literary Annual, Ruby, Slipstream, Tikkun,* and *Washington Review.*

"Silk," "The Stammer," "The Weekly Loaf," "He Enters Berlin through the Rosenthal Gate" (as "Moses Mendelssohn Enters Berlin through the Rosenthal Gate"), and "Yiddish" first appeared in *Poetry.*

"The Break," "The Grin," "The Ghetto Raised Me" (as "He Leaves the Ghetto"), "The Bowl on My Back" (as "The Hump"), "An Israelite in Whom There Is No Guile" (as "The Lavater Affair"), "Abraham at *Morgenstunden*" (as "*Morgenstunden*"), "A Purchase of Porcelain," and "The Stranger from Dessau" first appeared in *Prairie Schooner.*

A selection of poems in this book won the Kinloch Rivers chapbook competition and appeared in an edition of 200 under the title *A Purchase of Porcelain.* An earlier version of this book was translated into Hebrew by Moshe Dor and published in Israel by Carmel Press.

NOTES

The translation of Mendelssohn's letter to Thomas Abbt in "Death Has Knocked at My Door" is from Sebastian Hensel's *The Mendelssohn Family.*

The epigraph to "The Stranger from Dessau" is from Herbert Kupferberg's *The Mendelssohns: Three Generations of Genius.*

JEAN NORDHAUS studied philosophy at Barnard College and received her doctorate in modern German literature from Yale University.

Her book-length poetry collection, *My Life in Hiding* (1991), appeared in the *Quarterly Review of Literature* series. She is also the author of *A Bracelet of Lies* (Washington Writers' Publishing House, 1987) and two chapbooks, *A Language of Hands* (SCOP, 1982) and *A Purchase of Porcelain*, which was published by the Poetry Society of South Carolina in May 1998.

MORE POETRY FROM MILKWEED EDITIONS

To order books or for more information, contact Milkweed at (800) 520-6455 or visit our website (www.milkweed.org).

TURNING OVER THE EARTH
Ralph Black

OUTSIDERS:
POEMS ABOUT REBELS, EXILES, AND RENEGADES
Edited by Laure-Anne Bosselaar

URBAN NATURE:
POEMS ABOUT WILDLIFE IN THE CITY
Edited by Laure-Anne Bosselaar

DRIVE, THEY SAID:
POEMS ABOUT AMERICANS AND THEIR CARS
Edited by Kurt Brown

NIGHT OUT:
POEMS ABOUT HOTELS, MOTELS, RESTAURANTS, AND BARS
Edited by Kurt Brown and Laure-Anne Bosselaar

VERSE AND UNIVERSE:
POEMS ABOUT SCIENCE AND MATHEMATICS
Edited by Kurt Brown

ASTONISHING WORLD:
SELECTED POEMS OF ÁNGEL GONZÁLEZ
Translated from the Spanish by Steven Ford Brown

MIXED VOICES:
CONTEMPORARY POEMS ABOUT MUSIC
Edited by Emilie Buchwald and Ruth Roston

THIS SPORTING LIFE:
POEMS ABOUT SPORTS AND GAMES
Edited by Emilie Buchwald and Ruth Roston

THE PHOENIX GONE, THE TERRACE EMPTY
Marilyn Chin

TWIN SONS OF DIFFERENT MIRRORS
Jack Driscoll and Bill Meissner

INVISIBLE HORSES
Patricia Goedicke

THE ART OF WRITING:
LU CHI'S *WEN FU*
Translated from the Chinese by Sam Hamill

BOXELDER BUG VARIATIONS
Bill Holm

THE DEAD GET BY WITH EVERYTHING
Bill Holm

BUTTERFLY EFFECT
Harry Humes

THE FREEDOM OF HISTORY
Jim Moore

THE LONG EXPERIENCE OF LOVE
Jim Moore

FIREKEEPER:
NEW AND SELECTED POEMS
Pattiann Rogers

SONG OF THE WORLD BECOMING:
NEW AND COLLECTED POEMS 1981–2001
Pattiann Rogers

WHITE FLASH/BLACK RAIN:
WOMEN OF JAPAN RELIVE THE BOMB
Edited by Lequita Vance-Watkins and Aratani Mariko

MILKWEED EDITIONS publishes with the intention of making a humane impact on society, in the belief that literature is a transformative art uniquely able to convey the essential experiences of the human heart and spirit. To that end, Milkweed publishes distinctive voices of literary merit in handsomely designed, visually dynamic books, exploring the ethical, cultural, and esthetic issues that free societies need continually to address. Milkweed Editions is a not-for-profit press.

JOIN US

Since its genesis as *Milkweed Chronicle* in 1979, Milkweed has helped hundreds of emerging writers reach their readers. Thanks to the generosity of foundations and of individuals like you, Milkweed Editions is able to continue its nonprofit mission of publishing books chosen on the basis of literary merit—on how they impact the human heart and spirit—rather than on how they impact the bottom line. That's a miracle that our readers have made possible.

In addition to purchasing Milkweed books, you can join the growing community of Milkweed supporters. Individual contributions of any amount are both meaningful and welcome. Contact us for a Milkweed catalog or log on to www.milkweed.org and click on "About Milkweed," then "Why Join Milkweed," to find out about our donor program, or simply call (800) 520-6455 and ask about becoming one of Milkweed's contributors. As a nonprofit press, Milkweed belongs to you, the community. Milkweed's board, its staff, and especially the authors whose careers you help launch thank you for reading our books and supporting our mission in any way you can.

Interior design by Dale Cooney
Typeset in Centaur MT
by Stanton Publication Services
Printed on acid-free 55# Glatfelter Writers paper
by Sheridan Books, Inc.